Book 2

Simply Classic
Orchestral and Operatic Masterworks

18 Favorite "Simpl

Margaret Goldston

Foreword

Similar to my *Simply Classics*, Books 1 and 2 and *Simply Classics Orchestral and Operatic Masterworks*, Book 1, this collection of piano arrangements features simplified excerpts of well-known orchestral and operatic works by the master composers. Written especially for early intermediate piano students, this book contains selections in a variety of styles that are representative of the various periods throughout the history of music. I have particularly made a special effort to arrange some of the works not usually included in simplified classical piano collections.

Students who can "hardly wait to play the classics" should have a pleasant time getting acquainted with these famous masterworks.

This collection is dedicated with appreciation to Paul Newlin, who assisted me with researching and selecting the music.

Contents

ISBN 0-7390-1232-0

He Shall Feed His Flock

from *The Messiah*

George Frideric Handel
Arr. by Margaret Goldston

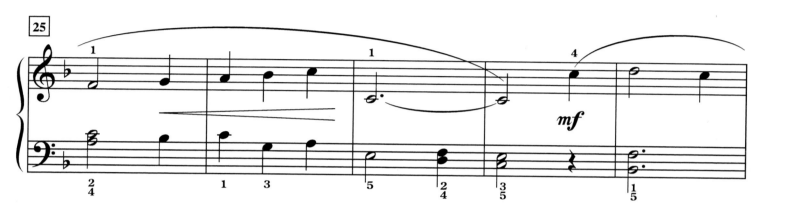

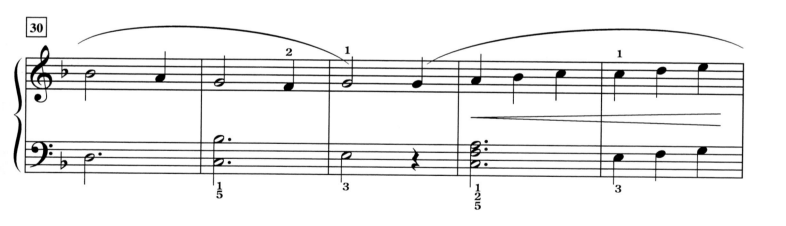

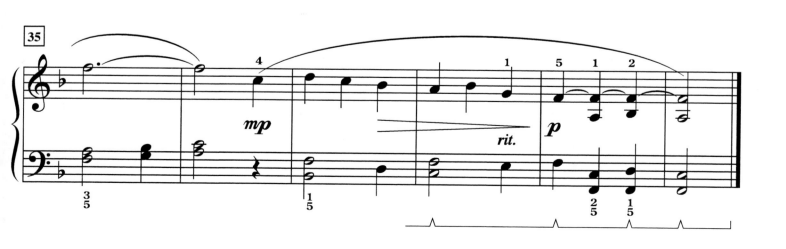

Sheep May Safely Graze

from the *Birthday Cantata*

Johann Sebastian Bach

Arr. by Margaret Goldston

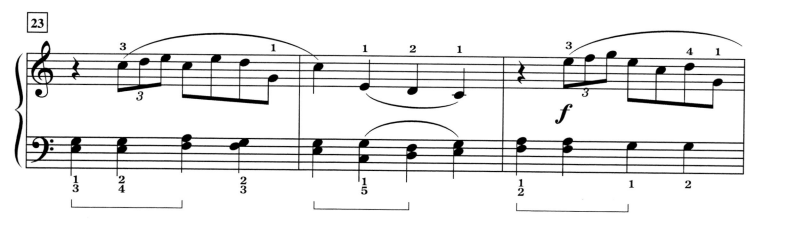

Piano Concerto in F Minor

Theme from the Second Movement

Johann Sebastian Bach
Arr. by Margaret Goldston

Largo con espressivo

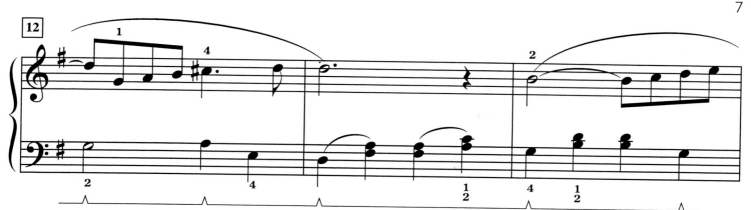

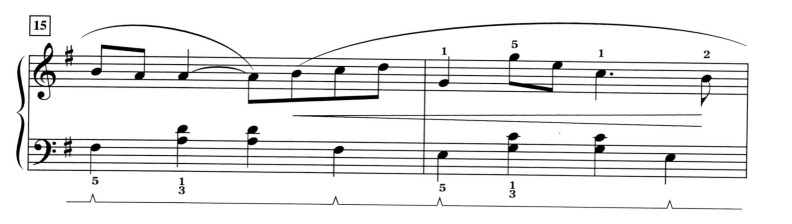

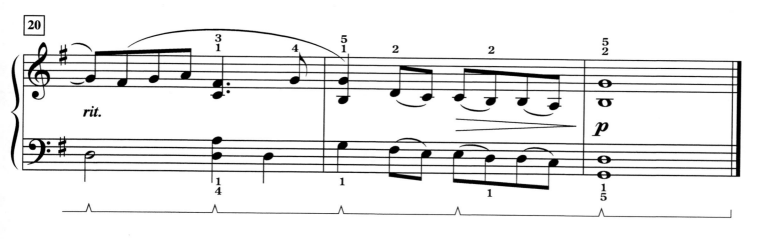

Symphony No. 6, Op. 68

Themes from the First Movement

Ludwig van Beethoven

Arr. by Margaret Goldston

Piano Concerto No. 3, Op. 37

Themes from the First Movement

Ludwig van Beethoven
Arr. by Margaret Goldston

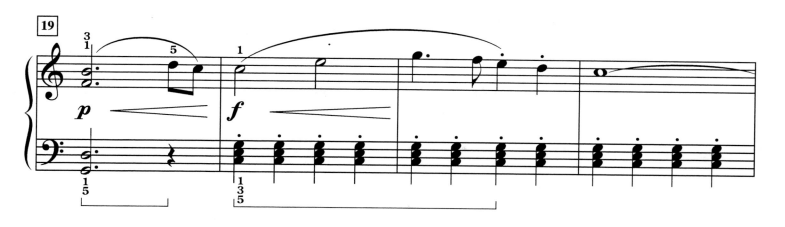

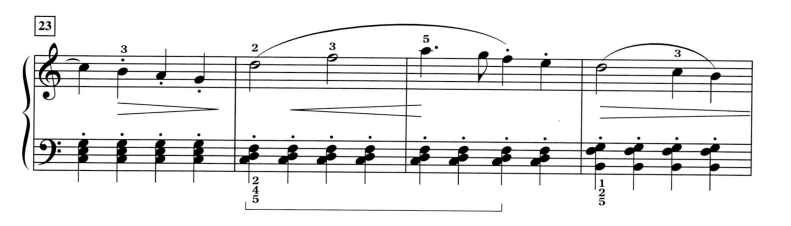

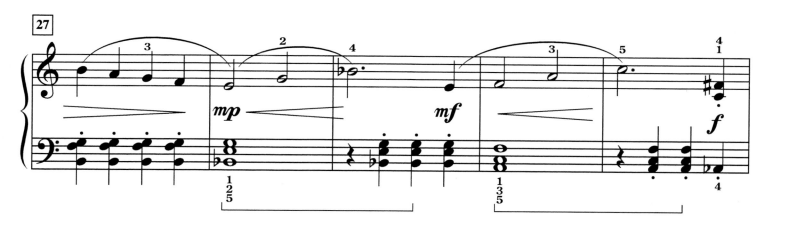

D. C. al Fine

Là ci darem la mano
(Give Me Your Hand, My Darling)
from *Don Giovanni*

Wolfgang Amadeus Mozart

Arr. by Margaret Goldston

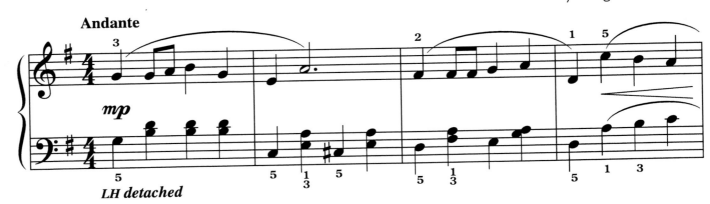

Variations on a Theme of Haydn

Johannes Brahms
Arr. by Margaret Goldston

Ballet Music

from *Rosamunde*

Franz Schubert
Arr. by Margaret Goldston

Egyptian Ballet Dance

from *Samson and Delilah*

Camille Saint-Saëns
Arr. by Margaret Goldston

Danse Macabre

Camille Saint-Saëns
Arr. by Margaret Goldston

Barcarolle

from *Tales of Hoffman*

Jacques Offenbach
Arr. by Margaret Goldston

Symphony in D Minor

Themes from the First Movement

César Franck

Arr. by Margaret Goldston

Aragonaise

from *Carmen*

Georges Bizet

Arr. by Margaret Goldston

Habañera

from *Carmen*

Georges Bizet
Arr. by Margaret Goldston

Piano Concerto No. 1, Op. 23

Theme from the First Movement

Peter Ilyich Tchaikovsky
Arr. by Margaret Goldston

Un bel dì
(One Fine Day)
from *Madama Butterfly*

Giacomo Puccini

Arr. by Margaret Goldston

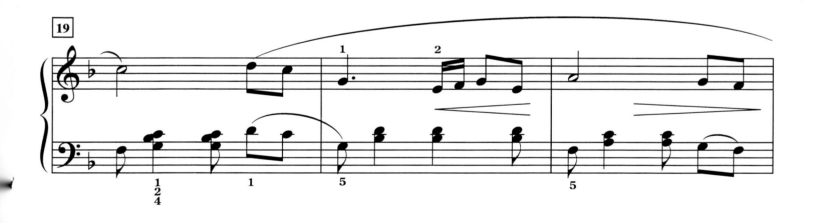

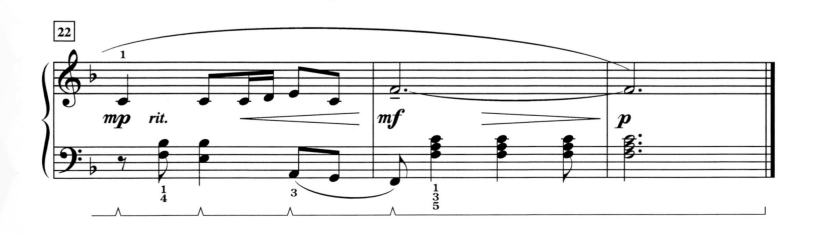

Praeludium

from the *Holberg Suite*

Edvard Grieg
Arr. by Margaret Goldston

Jupiter, the Bringer of Jollity

from *The Planets*

Gustav Holst

Arr. by Margaret Goldston